Face to Face Communication

Making Human Connections in a Technology-Driven World

Kathleen A. Begley, Ed.D.

A Crisp Fifty-Minute™ Series Book

This Fifty-Minute™ Book is designed to be "read with a pencil." It is an excellent workbook for self-study as well as classroom learning. All material is copyright-protected and cannot be duplicated without permission from the publisher. *Therefore, be sure to order a copy for every training participant through our Web site, www.axzopress.com.*

Face to Face Communication
Making Human Connections in a Technology-Driven World

Kathleen A. Begley, Ed.D.

CREDITS:

VP, Product Development:	**Charlie Blum**
Editor:	**Ann Gosch**
Production Editor:	**Genevieve McDermott**
Design	**Nicole Phillips**
Production Artist:	**Rich Lehl**

ISBN 10: 1-56052-699-8
ISBN 13: 978-1-56052-6995
Library of Congress Catalog Card Number 2004108525
Printed in the United States of America
3 4 5 10 09

Learning Objectives for

FACE TO FACE COMMUNICATION

The learning objectives for *Face to Face Communication* are listed below. They have been developed to guide the user to the core issues covered in this book.

The objectives of this book are to help the user:

1) Learn the unique power of and continuing need for face-to-face communication in an electronic age

2) Understand that nonverbal communication is a key part of getting your message across to your audience

3) Learn how to use words to create positive relationships and resolve conflicts

4) Discover how to foster an attitude that good listening is one of the most important factors in human interaction

5) Explore adapting face-to-face communication principles to other communication when time and costs prevent you from meeting in person

Assessing Progress

A Crisp Series **assessment** is available for this book. The 25-item, multiple-choice and true/false questionnaire allows the reader to evaluate his or her comprehension of the subject matter.

To download the assessment and answer key, go to www.axzopress.com and search on the book title.

Assessments should not be used in any employee-selection process.

About the Author

Dr. Kathleen A. Begley, owner of Write Company Plus in West Chester, Pennsylvania, is a full-time professional speaker and writer. Every day, she uses face-to-face communication to convey her messages to business audiences.

Kathleen has provided communications training in all 50 states of the United States as well as in Asia and Europe. Her audiences have included professionals from most Fortune 500 companies.

She has authored three previous books: *Deadline, Writing That Sells,* and *The ABCs of Entrepreneurship. Writing That Sells,* written for business people in any occupation who want to write more persuasively, is a Crisp Series book by Thomson Learning.

Listed in several editions of *Who's Who,* Kathleen holds a doctoral degree in business education from Wilmington College. She received her bachelor's degree in English from Temple University and her master's in political science from Villanova University.

Kathleen believes that outstanding performance in face-to-face communication is the No. 1 requirement for career success, even in this high-tech age. Technophiles, listen up! Kathleen is a firm subscriber to the theory that it is not what you say, but how you say it.

She says she has learned a lot about nonverbal communication by watching her dogs interact with her and each other. "When I come home from a trip," Kathleen says, "Hershey, Panda, and Spike never actually *say,* 'I missed you and I'm glad you are home.' But I sure get that message when they greet me at the door with their wagging tails and expectant faces."

Kathleen would love to have face-to-face conversations with all of her readers. But that is impossible. So she will gladly settle for getting your comments and questions over the Internet. Send her an e-mail at Kbegley@writecompanyplus.com.

Preface

Several decades ago, in his mega best-seller *Megatrends: Ten New Directions Transforming Our Lives,* John Naisbitt introduced a concept called "high tech, high touch." His notion in 1962 was that as human beings became capable of anonymous electronic communication, they would concurrently need more close-up personal interaction.

His forecast has come to pass.

At a time when coffee lovers can make cappuccino in their own kitchens, they still flock to cafes where they can sip a latte and talk with others. Starbucks, a worldwide business phenomenon of the recent past, has made its fortune partly on this need for human togetherness.

While many children spend hours in solitary play with video games, people are buying and playing more family-round-the-table games such as Scrabble and Monopoly. The Game Manufacturers Association, an industry trade group, reported in 2003 that board games sales were increasing an astonishing 20% per year.

When natural and man-made disasters unfold on CNN, horrified viewers seek out in-person opportunities to share their grief and gather information. Who could forget the sight of the pilgrimages to makeshift shrines following accidents such as Princess Diana's car crash or John F. Kennedy Jr.'s downed plane?

In the 21st century, men and women continually lurch between the impersonal nature of technology and the intimate reality of human relationships.

There are many situations—often those involving escalating conflict, sensitive feelings, high priority, important authority, or a great deal of money—that demand business people take the time and trouble to get into the same room to exchange information. Or at least they try to *simulate* face-to-face communication when individuals are in remote locations.

Make no mistake about it. Face-to-face communication skills remain one of the primary roads to career success, even in this computer age.

"Most communication is carried out face-to-face with other individuals: asking for information, offering advice, your annual performance appraisal, or telling someone what you think of their performance—all tend to be done in a one-to-one situation. This is one of the most critical areas of communication to get right," says Chris Roebuck in *Effective Communication.*

In other words, if you are a typical business person today, you probably need to take a serious look at your communications methods. Are you e-mailing more and meeting less for financial reasons? Or as some psychologists believe, are you avoiding human contact mostly because of a lack of interpersonal skills?

If the latter, you may be sorry.

In a conversationally written, colorfully designed business book *Re-imagine!* published in 2004, internationally known business guru Tom Peters says unequivocally that you should constantly attend to your face-to-face communication. Not to do so, he says, will lead to career disaster.

"We believe in high tech, high touch," Peters writes. "No question, technology is the Great Enabler. But, paradoxically, now the human bit is more, not less, important than ever before."

Because of the pressures of time and resources in a highly competitive economy, you may be one of the millions of men and women who recently have been giving minimal attention to face-to-face communication.

Is it not faster, you may argue, to make a quick phone call, send a brief e-mail, or hook up via videoconferencing to have a meeting of the minds?

Yes, and no.

"The modern office is full of fancy gadgets—computers and the Internet, uplinks and downlinks, videoconferencing, and online databases," writes Sheida Hodge in *Global Smarts: The Art of Communicating and Deal Making Anywhere in the World.* "Many people think they should let the fancy technology handle the messy task of interfacing with people."

To be sure, electronic and written communications work fine in the majority of situations: routine messages, emergency directives, mass mailings. But relying solely on technology can backfire dramatically in situations that cry out for a human touch.

In her book *Reading People,* author Jo-Ellan Dimitrius alludes to the propensity of young, technically oriented employees to communicate largely in computer chat rooms. "If you want to become a better communicator, you must make a conscious effort to engage other people (in person)," she writes. "Even the most entrenched Internet junkie can learn the true meaning of 'chat' if the desire is there, but you have to get off the couch and make it happen."

The purpose of this book is to help you recognize and deal with this modern business communication paradox.

Kathleen A. Begley

Kathleen A. Begley

Table of Contents

Appendix 81

Face the Facts

> "Consistent, daily face-to-face communication promotes more than just good feelings; it also promotes effective and collaborative teamwork."

–Gary McClain and Deborah Romaine,
The Everything Managing People Book

Recognize Face-to-Face Impact

Face-to-face communication? How old-fashioned!

In this computerized age, you may be wondering why you should improve your in-person communication. After all, most businesses seem to do 99% of communication by telephone, teleconferencing, videoconferencing, e-mail, and on rare occasions, snail mail.

But they are wrong to do so.

In *Managing Face-to-Face Communication: Survival Tactics for People and Products in the 21st Century,* Allen Ivey underscores the importance of good interpersonal skills. He reports that a recent study recording what managers do during the day found more than 500 separate interactions with colleagues, subordinates, superiors, and clients during a single working day.

"As is well known," Ivey writes, "many firings occur because of interpersonal difficulties, most often relating to communication failures. Stories of time, sales, and money lost due to failure to listen or communicate information are legion." And these failures often begin when you try to send by telephone or e-mail a critical message.

Face-to-face communication remains the most powerful human interaction. As wonderful as electronic devices are, they can never fully replace the intimacy and immediacy of people conversing in the same room.

For best interaction, it often is helpful to go back to the basics and get face-to-face. Why? It works. And it has worked for millions of years. Thousands of experts say definitively that the best communication occurs when a speaker and a listener are in the same room.

"Eye contact, facial expressions, body movements, space, time, distance, appearance—all these nonverbal clues influence the way the message is interpreted, or decoded, by the receiver," writes Mary Ellen Guffey in *Business Communication: Process and Product.*

Unconvinced? Just think about how often English speakers allude to the word face in everyday communication. In dozens of ways, people use this term to convey a variety of important ideas. Face it: Face-to-face communication is here to stay, despite your ability to circumvent it with a wide variety of electronic methods.

FACE THE EXPRESSIONS

From the following list of idioms, fill in the blanks in the statements below to make these common expressions complete.

- ➤ The nose on your face
- ➤ Get out of my face
- ➤ Face time
- ➤ Face value
- ➤ Poker face
- ➤ About face
- ➤ Straight face
- ➤ Saving face
- ➤ Flat on her face
- ➤ Facial expressions
- ➤ Face-to-face
- ➤ Face the music
- ➤ Best face
- ➤ Two-faced

1. Salespeople put a high value on _____ with prospects.

2. You might tell an aggressive co-worker to _____.

3. Seeing the humor in the situation, the human resource manager nevertheless tried to keep a _____.

4. The once eager job applicant did an _____ and turned down the job.

5. In crisis, a team can be more effective when discussing solutions in a _____ meeting.

6. The _____ of the contract is $100,000.

7. The new employee feared falling _____.

CONTINUED

CONTINUED

8. _____ are a powerful nonverbal.

9. In general, Asian executives put a high value on _____.

10. The engineer told the technician he was _____ for talking behind his back.

11. For her egregious mistake, the administrative assistant knew she would have to _____.

12. The manager wanted to put the _____ on declining sales.

13. Ethical accounting should make a company's value as plain as _____.

14. While negotiating with an uncompromising client, the saleswoman kept a _____.

Compare your answers to the author's responses in the Appendix.

Appreciate the Advantages

Simply put, *face-to-face communication* means the exchanging of information, thoughts, and feelings when the participants are in the same physical space.

Face-to-face communication occurs in a wide range of business activities, including formal meetings, coffee room chitchat, hallway encounters, one-on-one coaching, annual evaluations, job interviews, and more. Face-to-face communication depends on the meeting of eyeballs rather than the meeting of modem and Internet connection.

Face-to-face communication is, in effect, a relationship. In their book *Secrets of Face-to-Face Communication,* Peter Bender and Robert Tracz write, "When you are communicating with another individual, you are in a short-term partnership with that person."

Of course, in this global age, it is sometimes too expensive to fly the staff to a central location. But even when that is the case, the best professionals simulate face-to-face communication through clever use of the technology at hand.

Although electronic communication is nearly miraculous for many types of business interchange, it fails miserably in situations involving high levels of the following elements:

➤ **Conflict:** When people are extremely upset, it is almost impossible to cool down the situation long distance.

Example: You need to stop continual bickering among workers at three industrial plants. You arrange a special off-site meeting at a convenient time for first-, second-, and third-shift workers at each location.

➤ **Emotion:** Employees in great emotional distress respond more positively to in-person contact than to electrically transmitted messages.

Example: You just learned a colleague's mother has died. You take the time to go to her cubicle and extend your sympathy.

➤ **Priority:** The situation involves the rollout of a product essential to the success of the company and the team—which needs to get together in the same room.

Example: You want to motivate the team to get the project done on time and on budget. You ask team members to have daily in-person status meetings until they finish the job.

➤ **Title:** Sometimes, for political reasons, it is wise to concede to the request of a high-level person to get together.

Example: Your manager wants you to fly across the country for what you consider a useless conference. You go anyway.

➤ **Money:** If a large internal or external client makes a request, face-to-face communication is the kind most likely to retain or expand the account.

Example: A client worth $5 million of business wants you to attend a sports event with him on the weekend. Even though you would prefer to spend that time with your family, you enthusiastically accompany the customer.

RECALL YOUR OWN ENCOUNTERS

Think about incidents in your own career where a face-to-face meeting would have turned around—or did turn around—communication that was getting out of control. Write examples in the five categories:

1. Conflict

_____

_____

2. Emotion

_____

_____

3. Priority

_____

_____

4. Title

_____

_____

5. Money

_____

_____

See the author's comments in the Appendix.

For more information about handling conflict and other difficult situations, read *Conflict Mangement,* by Herbert Kindler, a Crisp Series book by Thomson Learning.

SEND YOUR MESSAGE

Read the following list of common workplace communications. Check (✓) those you think could be best handled face-to-face rather than by telephone, teleconferencing, videoconferencing, or e-mail.

❑   1. Announcement of a company merger

❑   2. Confirmation of a routine appointment

❑   3. Counseling about an employee's suspected drinking problem

❑   4. Apology for being late to give your speech

❑   5. Last-minute negotiations between union and management

❑   6. Distribution of information to 5,000 people about the annual company picnic

❑   7. Resolution of a multiyear conflict between factory workers

❑   8. Coaching on time management for a chronically late employee

❑   9. Loan application to a bank

❑ 10. Persuading an important employee not to quit on the spot

❑ 11. Conference of people in remote locations

❑ 12. Request from your CEO to meet about a pet peeve important only to her

Compare your answers to the author's responses in the Appendix.

Understand the Behaviors

Like all communication, face-to-face involves a sender and a receiver. There usually is a give and take of roles. You take turns *talking,* which is sending, and *listening,* which is receiving.

As the sender, you have a great deal of control. Knowing that many people get negative impressions about speakers who cross their arms, you may force yourself to avoid this behavior. When receiving communication, however, you should ask for clarification about apparent word/body language contradictions. If you see someone grimacing while lifting a computer, for example, you might think he has a muscular pain. But you might be wrong. When you ask the person, you learn he has an abscessed tooth.

Verbal vs. Nonverbal Communication

Face-to-face behaviors have two important elements: verbal and nonverbal. To get your point across the best, you need to master both.

Nonverbal communication includes these five factors:

➤ Body language

➤ Physical appearance

➤ Voice quality

➤ Your respect for time

➤ Spatial arrangements

Verbal communication includes these three elements:

➤ Vocabulary

➤ Organization and structure of words into sentences

➤ Use of overall grammar and syntax

Astonishing as it may seem, verbal communication accounts for only 8% of communication. Nonverbals are responsible for the remaining 92%. Amazed by the lopsidedness? Perhaps you are thinking of aspects of your voice as verbal. But they are not. *Verbal* applies only to words. Activity involving the mouth that does not involve words is termed *oral.* Chewing gum, for example, is an oral activity, but not a verbal one.

Ironically, as insignificant as your words may seem from the statistics, it is a mistake to minimize verbal communication. Think about the difference if someone tells you "you must move that box" vs. "I need you to move that box for safety reasons." The second sentence starts with "I" instead of "You," uses the neutral verb "need," and provides a benefit for the listener. These three elements of verbal communication—all words—make your statement more persuasive.

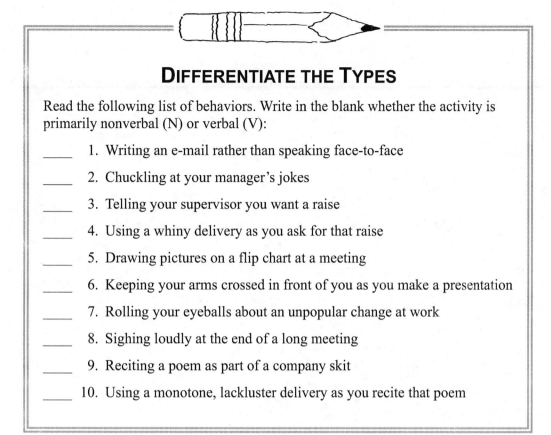

DIFFERENTIATE THE TYPES

Read the following list of behaviors. Write in the blank whether the activity is primarily nonverbal (N) or verbal (V):

_____ 1. Writing an e-mail rather than speaking face-to-face

_____ 2. Chuckling at your manager's jokes

_____ 3. Telling your supervisor you want a raise

_____ 4. Using a whiny delivery as you ask for that raise

_____ 5. Drawing pictures on a flip chart at a meeting

_____ 6. Keeping your arms crossed in front of you as you make a presentation

_____ 7. Rolling your eyeballs about an unpopular change at work

_____ 8. Sighing loudly at the end of a long meeting

_____ 9. Reciting a poem as part of a company skit

_____ 10. Using a monotone, lackluster delivery as you recite that poem

Compare your answers to the author's responses in the Appendix.

Conquer Your Fears

Despite all evidence of the value of having senders and receivers of important messages in the same room, many people often resist getting face-to-face with managers, co-workers, and customers. Common excuses: They do not have time to go to a face-to-face meeting. They do not have the money to travel across the country. They do not have the linguistic ability to comprehend a counterpart's accent.

All of these rationales may be valid.

But the bigger truth is that face-to-face communication takes courage. It is not easy to confront an angry customer, speak to a large group, or get the attention of a high-level executive in the hallway.

It is essential for you to acknowledge anxiety when you are deciding whether to deal with an interpersonal action face-to-face. It may be helpful to buttress yourself by thinking of FACE as an acronym for the following actions:

Face your fear about communicating with people in the same room rather than on the same intranet.

Act in the manner that will produce the best results—not necessarily the fastest and easiest.

Choose face-to-face communication if you are torn between two channels; think of in-person contact as your *default*.

Engage the receiver through your effective use of nonverbal and verbal techniques.

Factor in Personality Preferences

To be sure, face-to-face communication is more comfortable and less stressful for some people than for others. The reason lies in innate personality differences.

According to the Myers-Briggs Type Indicator (MBTI), a well-known instrument measuring personality differences, human beings differ on four levels. The popular MBTI, taken by millions of people around the world, says most people are closer to one end of each of these four scales:

> ➤ **Introversion/Extroversion**

> ➤ **Sensing/Intuiting**

> ➤ **Thinking/ Feeling**

> ➤ **Judging/Perceiving**

As a scientific instrument, MBTI's descriptors mean different things than the same words used in everyday conversation. *Introversion,* for example, does not denote a shy and reserved person, nor does *extroversion* denote someone outgoing and gregarious. Here is a fuller explanation of each term as used in this popular measurement tool:

> ➤ **Introversion:** Gaining strength from inner contemplation such as time alone, quiet time, or meditation
> ➤ **Extroversion:** Getting energy from outside stimuli such as other people, films, or performances

> ➤ **Sensing:** Paying attention to details and the here-and-now
> ➤ **Intuiting:** Seeing the big picture and future possibilities

> ➤ **Thinking:** Operating primarily from logic when making important choices
> ➤ **Feeling:** Factoring emotional impact heavily into life-changing decisions

> ➤ **Judging:** Liking orderliness and predictability even amid chaos
> ➤ **Perceiving:** Being easily able to adapt to changing circumstances

KNOW THYSELF

Wondering what your preferences are? Take this brief, nonscientific quiz to get some hints:

1. After a long day at a business conference, I would most likely:

   a) Go to my room and watch TV
   b) Join others for dinner in a nearby restaurant

2. I usually like art that:

   a) Shows people, places, and things as they look in real life, as in Renoir
   b) Is avant-garde and only symbolic of its subject matter, as in Picasso

3. If asked to expatriate to another country for a few years, the first thing I would do is to:

   a) Figure out the tax and other costs or savings involved in relocating abroad
   b) Ask my spouse and children their feelings about such a radical change

4. If it were true to my nature, my clothes closet at home would contain:

   a) Neatly pressed outfits arranged by color on wooden hangers
   b) A pile of dirty laundry on the floor

As you may have guessed, "A" answers correspond in exact order to introversion, sensing, thinking, and judging. "B" answers stand for extroversion, intuiting, feeling, and perceiving.

The tie-in with face-to-face communication is that people who choose mostly "A" answers probably are by nature less comfortable with interpersonal contact than their counterparts who choose "B" answers. Think about it:

➤ *Extroverts* enjoy the stimulation of interaction more than *Introverts*.

➤ *Intuitors* view face-to-face interaction as part of the quest for success while *Sensors* may see it as an interruption in daily activities.

➤ *Feelers* are more comfortable than *Thinkers* with in-person expression of emotion, both positive and negative.

➤ *Perceivers* are easily able to go with the flow—and uncertainty—inherent in any live interaction. The unpredictability often worries *Judgers*.

Still, even introverted, sensing, thinking, judging individuals can learn effective face-to-face behaviors if their career depends on it. And it probably does.

CASE STUDY: Analyze Others' Behavior

Read the following scenario. Write your answers to the questions on the lines provided.

Frank is a highly educated computer professional. At age 26, he has devoted his educational pursuits exclusively to computer technology. He has a master's degree in electrical engineering from a top-tier college. He wants to climb as high as he can on the corporate ladder.

Unfortunately, Frank has not had the time to develop his interpersonal skills. Feeling the lack, he often telephones and e-mails people who are in the same building and even on the same floor. He finds people contact unsettling.

Frank envies Alison and Ellis, two of his co-workers. They are in their early 30s and seem to have a good grasp of both technical and nontechnical abilities required for success in the 21st century. The last time Alison and Ellis gave a presentation about their current project, Frank was amazed how comfortable and relaxed they both seemed.

In his last performance review, Frank's manager told him he needed to improve his communication skills if he wanted to be promoted in the company

1. To whom could Frank turn to face his fear?

   _____

   _____

2. What other kinds of action could Frank use to improve his face-to-face communication?

   _____

   _____

3. Why should Frank choose to devote time and effort to his interpersonal skills?

   _____

   _____

4. How could Frank practice engaging other people in a safe, nonwork setting?

   _____

   _____

Compare your answers to the author's responses in the Appendix.

Review

Put a check (✓) in the box next to the ideas from this part that you plan to use in your work life:

❑ Get out of my office when possible and talk to other people in person.

❑ Weigh the importance of a situation when deciding whether to meet face-to-face.

❑ Use nonverbal and verbal communication effectively.

❑ Overcome my anxiety about getting face-to-face, especially with difficult people.

❑ Factor in my innate personality preferences when figuring out how much I will need to stretch to communicate face-to-face more often and more effectively.

Practice Your

Nonverbals

> *Face-to-face networking is a powerful and valuable tool; meeting people not only provides tangible help, but also helps to clarify one's thinking, providing perspective and a positive approach."*
>
> —**Martha Finney**, *Find Your Calling, Love Your Life*

Value the Unspoken

"Nonverbal communication—communication that does not use words—takes place all the time," writes Kitty Locker in *Business and Administrative Communication.* "Smiles, frowns, who sits where at a meeting, the size of the office, how long someone keeps a visitor waiting—all these communicate pleasure or anger, friendliness or distance, power and status."

Animals are particularly talented senders of nonverbal messages. If you have been around a friendly dog, you have experienced the animal's pushing its head under your hand. The message is crystal clear without words. "Pet me," the dog seems to be saying.

Check the Lexicon

Even if only on an intuitive level, both ancient and modern societies have recognized the superior power of action over words. That is why aphorisms throughout the ages and across many cultures have touched on the importance of nonverbal communication. See if you can fill in the blanks in the following adages.

1. It's not what you say, but _____.

2. A picture is worth _____.

3. Show me _____.

4. Talk is _____.

5. Do as I say, not as _____.

6. The eyes are the window _____.

7. Actions speak louder than _____.

8. Put your money where _____.

9. It's time to fish or _____.

10. Put up or _____.

Compare your answers to the author's responses in the Appendix.

For more information on nonverbal communication, read *Communication Skills for Leaders,* by Bert Decker, a Crisp Series book by Thomson Learning.

Be Aware of Your Body

When people hear the term *nonverbal,* many immediately think of body language. Although it is only one factor in nonverbal communication, people will usually believe what they see in your face and manners more than what you tell them in words. So you need to develop skill in the use of body language to ensure that others receive the same message through their eyes as through their ears.

Translate These Gestures

Facial expressions and body movements can show enthusiasm or boredom, pleasure or pain, sincerity or sarcasm. Read this list of common gestures. Write on the blank line after each one how this form of body language might be interpreted by the average observer.

1. Scratching your nose

   _____

2. Pursing your lips

   _____

3. Pointing with a straight arm

   _____

4. Wringing hands

   _____

5. Pounding on the table with your fist

   _____

6. Winking

   _____

7. Playing with your hair

   _____

8. Sitting across the table from the other person

   _____

9. Making eye contact

   _____

10. Biting on pen

_____

11. Steepling with your hands

_____

12. Stepping out from behind a podium during a speech

_____

Compare your answers to the author's responses in the Appendix.

Check Your Physical Appearance

Your physical appearance can send unspoken messages just as surely as your body language. In their book *The Nonverbal Communication Reader: Classic and Contemporary Readings,* Laura Guerrero, Joseph DeVito, and Michael Hecht note that research shows that people perceive others differently according to body stereotypes. For example, people who are tall and thin are often considered by others to be nervous or intelligent. Men and women with short, round body types frequently are seen as friendly or lazy. Muscular individuals sometimes are thought to be energetic or ambitious.

As uncomfortable as this notion is for people of substance, many elements of looks and style contribute mightily to others' perceptions of you. They may even play a part in determining life outcomes.

Take an objective look at your personal appearance. Perhaps there is something about it that may be causing a problem in your business life. If so, consider changing or minimizing it, at least for the office. After all, it is acceptable to have different styles in your personal and professional lives, as the following examples demonstrate:

Hairstyle

Personal: You like your hair heavily sprayed to look spikey.
Professional: You ease up on the hairspray for a more natural style.

Grooming

Personal: You come from a culture that chooses not to mask body odor.
Professional: You use deodorant to prevent or mask a smell others may find unpleasant.

Cosmetics

Personal: You like the look of heavy eye makeup and lipstick.
Professional: You tone down cosmetics with neutral tones and matte finishes.

Tattoos

Personal: You have interesting tattoos on your arms and legs.
Professional: You wear long sleeves and pants to avoid offending co-workers.

Jewelry

Personal: You love dangling earrings and multiple necklaces and bracelets.
Professional: You choose more moderate jewelry to avoid distracting colleagues or sending a wrong message.

Clothing

Personal: You dress flamboyantly in the latest fashions.
Professional: You invest in more conservative clothing appropriate to your field of employment.

Hosiery

Personal: You rarely wear socks or hose in your personal life.
Professional: You cover your legs, even in warm weather.

Teeth

Personal: Your teeth have decayed because of poor dental care as a child.
Professional: You find a skilled cosmetic dentist.

Weight

Personal: You have been chubby since you were a child.
Professional: You wear colors and styles designed to minimize your girth.

Height

Personal: Your entire family is short and so are you.
Professional: You consider wearing heels or shoe inserts to add an inch or two, and you ensure that the other aspects of your appearance communicate the appropriate maturity and seriousness.

REMEMBER YOUR IMPRESSIONS

The impact of appearance goes even further than grooming and dress. If you look into recent history and popular culture, you will notice that many famous people have possessed one or more outstanding physical characteristics or habits that helped parlay them to fame or fortune. The following list includes famous people from the past from a variety of cultures. On the lines after the names, note how their looks affected their lives and careers.

1. Grace Kelly, who became Princess Grace of Monaco

_____

2. Winston Churchill

_____

3. Marilyn Monroe

_____

4. Mother Teresa

_____

5. Cary Grant

_____

6. John F. Kennedy

_____

7. Elvis Presley

_____

8. Princess Diana

_____

9. Henry VIII

_____

10. Buddha

_____

Compare your answers to the author's responses in the Appendix.

Take Advantage of Your Voice

Many people think that the voice is a minor consideration in communication. But this is far from the truth. Listeners get impressions and make inferences about you simply from the sound of your speech.

Unless you are a professional speaker or singer, you probably have had little, if any, voice training. But you can change many aspects of your voice to alter the meaning. The easiest to master are:

> ➤ **Volume:** How you increase and decrease your decibel level

> ➤ **Speed:** How you fit your words into time

> ➤ **Pitch:** How you access high and low notes

> ➤ **Tone:** How you sound to listeners—welcoming or unfriendly, confident or insecure, condescending or deferential, arrogant or humble

> ➤ **Enunciation:** How you pronounce letters or word forms such as "ing" in the middle of and at the end of words

> ➤ **Inflection:** How you say certain syllables or words a little louder and longer than others

You can train your voice to excel in all of these qualities if you listen closely to the way you speak and concentrate on improvement. The exercise that follows will demonstrate how different your message can be by varying each of these aspects.

UNDERSTAND THE IMPACT OF YOUR VOICE

Read the passages inside quotation marks in the following examples. Say exactly the same words each time, changing the vocal characteristic to fit each description noted. Observe how differently you come across.

Volume

A speaker walks into a training room. She is from out-of-town and has never met the participants. She says, "Welcome to this training session. We have planned an entertaining and informative session today."

Speech Quality	Listener Reaction	Listener Inference
Too Soft	I can't hear her.	She must be inexperienced.
Too Loud	I'm getting a headache.	She must be hard of hearing.
Just Right	I'm glad I came.	She is a skilled speaker.

Speed

A sales clerk has a long line of people at the cash register. He says, "I'll try to take care of everyone as soon as I can."

Speech Quality	Listener Reaction	Listener Inference
Too Fast	I couldn't catch it.	He's way too rushed.
Too Slow	I doubt his words.	He must be dim-witted.
Just Right	I'm calmed down.	He cares about customers.

Pitch

A young man is interviewing for a job. He says, "I know I can do all these tasks with a little training."

Speech Quality	Listener Reaction	Listener Inference
Too High	I sense inner conflict.	He's probably boasting.
Too Low	I think he seems fake.	He may manipulate with voice.
Just Right	I'll hire him.	He speaks well.

CONTINUED

Tone

An executive is visiting the United Kingdom. He meets one of his peers. He says, "I'd love to have dinner with you and your spouse. How about 7:30?"

Speech Quality	Listener Reaction	Listener Inference
Too Friendly	I'm uncomfortable.	He's a pushy American.
Too Unfriendly	I'm confused.	He sounds pompous.
Just Right	I like this man.	He would be nice to dine with.

Enunciation

A computer professional gives a status report. He says, "Believe me, we will have the programming finished on time and on budget."

Speech Quality	Listener Reaction	Listener Inference
Bad Enunciation	I can't understand him.	He needs speech therapy.
Exaggerated	I'm disconcerted.	He must think he's on stage.
Just Right	I can hear clearly.	He pronounced every syllable.

Inflection

Among the most interesting but elusive vocal traits is inflection, the changes in pitch or loudness in your voice as you speak. Read the following sentence five different ways by emphasizing the italicized word. Then write down the way the specific inflection changes the meaning.

1. *Vijay* is my wonderful manager.

   _____

2. Vijay *is* my wonderful manager.

   _____

3. Vijay is *my* wonderful manager.

   _____

4. Vijay is my *wonderful* manager.

   _____

5. Vijay is my wonderful *manager.*

   _____

Compare your answers to the author's responses in the Appendix.

Watch the Clock

Punctuality and efficient use of time is another form of nonverbal communication. It can convey your respect for others, your eagerness to be involved, or your seriousness about the matter at hand.

Consider what is communicated in these scenarios:

➤ Rambling for almost an hour proved embarrassing in 1988 for then Arkansas Governor and later U.S. President William Clinton when he made his first address to a Democratic National Convention. As the world news media reported the following day, Clinton received the loudest applause from the restless audience when he uttered the phrase: "In conclusion." By contrast, completing a presentation within the time allotted signals both respect for the audience's time and better preparation of the speech itself.

➤ Missing the deadline for completing an important work project is likely to communicate to your manager a lack of seriousness about the job, of respect for the team, or of organizational skills required to complete the work on time.

➤ Showing up three hours late for a social event, without having called with your reason for the delay, often sends a message that other things were more important and you did not really want to be there.

➤ Insisting that a one-on-one meeting take only five minutes could communicate different messages depending on the situation. Most often it would indicate that you do not consider the other person important enough to give him more than five minutes of your time. But a manager could stipulate the tight time frame as a learning tool, to compel her employee to hone his argument and make his point concisely.

➤ Being 10 minutes early for a job interview communicates that you are organized and eager for the job.

➤ Checking his watch while his debate opponent was speaking was the undoing of U.S. President George Bush during the 1992 Presidential debates. OK, so the other speaker was the extremely talkative Bill Clinton. Nevertheless, the media picked up on this nonverbal communication as a sign that the incumbent lacked the energy or enthusiasm for a second term. Many political analysts thought that it contributed to his loss of the election.

Time is viewed differently in other cultures, but it still communicates. According to Virginia Richmond and James McCroskey in *Nonverbal Behavior in Interpersonal Relations,* "For most Americans, it is unforgivable to be more than 15 minutes late for any appointment without a very good excuse." If you are chronically late in Germany, you may develop a reputation as being lazy and disorganized. On the other hand, if you are too rigid about scheduling in Mexico, you probably will be viewed as unfeeling and insensitive. In Russia, lateness may be tolerated from those in power, but not from lower-level workers. No matter what your culture, watch the clock to be sure your nonverbal communication matches the message you want to convey.

Consider Spatial Arrangements

Although most of the emphasis in nonverbal communication is on the appearance and behavior of the individuals themselves, increasing attention is being given to the influence of nonhuman factors on human transactions, according to Mark Knapp and Judith Hall in *Nonverbal Communication in Human Interaction.* They note that people arrange their environments to help them accomplish their communicative goals.

In what ways do you arrange or rearrange your environment to communicate a message? Consider what is being implied when you set up a room for training. Do you arrange chairs in a theater setting or in a horseshoe shape? Each of these spatial arrangements of people and objects communicates a nonverbal message about the level of interaction you are expecting or encouraging in the training session.

As people enter the training room, do you walk around and shake hands, or do you take a chair in the back of the room and sit down until it is time to start? Each of these behaviors communicates before you utter your first word.

Your position in your surroundings can communicate a range of messages without words. How do you react if you see someone exhibiting the following nonverbal behaviors?

➤ Flinching back as you approach

➤ Reaching out his hand in greeting

➤ Filing papers on the floor

➤ Pulling her chair to the same side of the table as her guest

➤ Getting up when you enter the room

➤ Walking away from you as he keeps talking

Think about what you might be communicating without knowing it—or without wanting to. Your own position and your arrangement of objects within your surroundings make a difference in your overall message.

Review

Put a check (✓) in the box next to the ideas from this part that you plan to use in your work life:

- ❑ Recognize the power of the unspoken.

- ❑ Use gestures and other body language appropriate to the situation.

- ❑ Improve my personal appearance and physical environment, such as my office.

- ❑ Practice changing different qualities of my voice, especially inflection.

- ❑ Respect the time constraints of my listeners.

- ❑ Convey the right messages through spatial arrangements.

Choose Your

Words Carefully

Too busy for face-to-face relationships? Nonsense. You have as many hours in the day as everyone else. Perfect your small-talk skills. They are the conduit through which strangers become acquaintances and acquaintances become friends."

– **Kathleen Brehony,** *Living a Connected Life*

Realize Your Words Have Impact

"Words matter. Words have meaning. Words have power to help or hinder, to instantly irritate or create cooperation, to confuse or to clarify," writes Kris Cole in *The Complete Idiot's Guide to Clear Communication.* "Depending on our purpose, we can choose words that are aggressive or compliant, neutral or emotive, clear or vague, courteous or challenging."

Make sure your words convey an image of power and self-confidence. You can do this by avoiding the common habits of justifying or minimizing your ideas with vague qualifiers and personal opinions. The following examples demonstrate how you can strengthen what you say and how you say it.

Example: *"I hate to interrupt, but I have an idea."*
Analysis: This statement makes you sound subservient to others at the meeting.
Revision: *"I'd like to interrupt with another idea."*

Example: *"I feel the budget is too high, don't you?"*
Analysis: Ending a sentence with a negative verb form minimizes your point.
Revision: *"I think the budget is too high."*

Example: *"I really admire the vice president."*
Analysis: This sentence is too vague and sounds as if you're fawning.
Revision: *"The vice president is a strong leader for change."*

Example: *"It seems to me that we should hire this applicant."*
Analysis: The first four words make you sound wishy-washy.
Revision: *"I believe strongly that we should hire this applicant."*

Example: *"It would be nice if we had a company cafeteria."*
Analysis: You will sound more confident if you state this idea as fact.
Revision: *"The company needs a cafeteria."*

Example: *"My new secretary is pretty good, really."*
Analysis: This compliment becomes meaningless because of excess qualifiers.
Revision: *"My new secretary is efficient."*

Example: *"Please do not hesitate to call."*
Analysis: This cliché plants a negative seed in the listener's mind.
Revision: *"Call me any time."*

Example: *"We trust that you will pay us on time."*
Analysis: Trust has nothing to do with your need for payments.
Revision: *"Please send your payment by the first of every month."*

Example: *"Should you want us to, we'll invoice you every month."*
Analysis: You need not base your billing on customer acceptance.
Revision: *"We will invoice you every month."*

Example: *"I didn't have much time to prepare this speech, but here goes…"*
Analysis: This admission will irritate your audience from the beginning.
Revision: *"I'm delighted to be here today to give this speech."*

On the world stage, political leaders and entertainment and sports celebrities have had specific quotations make or break their careers. The same thing can happen to you on a smaller scale, so make sure listeners remember your words in a positive, rather than a negative, light.

QUOTE ME ON THAT

Read the quotations below from well-known people from the past and present. In the blank space before each statement, indicate whether the statement contributed positively (P) or negatively (N) to the individual's public image.

___ 1. *"You can't shake hands with a clenched fist."*
—Indian Prime Minister Indira Gandhi

___ 2. *"Whoever said 'It's not whether you win or lose that counts' probably lost."* —Czechoslovakian-American tennis star Martina Navratilova

___ 3. *"If you bungle raising your children, I don't think whatever else you do well matters very much."* —Jacqueline Kennedy Onassis

___ 4. *"China is a big country, inhabited by many Chinese."*
—French President Charles De Gaulle

___ 5. *"Adventure is worthwhile in itself."* —American aviator Amelia Earhart

___ 6. *"Outside of the killings, Washington has one of the lowest crime rates in the country."* —Marion Barry, mayor of Washington, D.C.

___ 7. *"Old age is like a plane flying through a storm. Once you are aboard, there is nothing you can do."* —Israeli Prime Minister Golda Meir

___ 8. *"I think we should raise the age at which juveniles can have guns."*
—43rd U.S. President George W. Bush

___ 9. *"I've always tried to go a step past wherever people expected me to end up."* —American opera star Beverly Sills

___ 10. *"A woman is like a tea bag. You never know how strong she is until she gets in hot water."* —former U.S. First Lady Eleanor Roosevelt

___ 11. *"Doing the best at this moment puts you into the best place for the next moment."* —American talk-show host Oprah Winfrey

___ 12. *"You know, in China they say, 'The thinner the chopsticks, the higher the social status.' Of course, I got the thinnest I could find. That's why people hate me."* —American entrepreneur Martha Stewart

___ 13. *"I'm astonished by people who take 18 years to write something. That's how long it took that guy to write* Madame Bovary, *and was that ever a best-seller?"* —American actor and *Rocky* scriptwriter Sylvester Stallone

___ 14. *"I want to be alone."* —Greta Garbo, Swedish movie actress

Compare your answers to the author's responses in the Appendix.

Create a Positive Impression

Words carry a variety of meanings, some denotative as defined in dictionaries and some connotative as used in daily conversation. The choice of one word over another can create a different impression.

Imagine that you are in a conversation with your manager about a co-worker you think is trying to take over your duties. You might be tempted to exclaim, "I know that creep is gunning for my job." But you would be better off saying "I think Joe is sabotaging me to promote his own career."

Look at the pairs of words below. The words in each pair have similar meanings. Yet you will probably agree that the words in the right-hand column seem harsher or more negative than those on the left.

Estimate	Guess
Negotiate	Haggle
State	Claim
Curious	Nosy
Cautious	Rigid
Woman	Chick
Flexible	Wishy-Washy
Policy	Rules
Old	Ancient
Absent-minded	Crazy
Spirited	Wild
Inexpensive	Cheap

In business communication, avoid negative words and expressions and instead maintain a positive, tactful, and courteous tone.

SPEAK POSITIVELY

For each word in the left-hand column below, think of a word that, in context, probably would strike your listener in a more positive way. Write this word on the corresponding line in the right-hand column.

1. Nit-picky   _____

2. Fight   _____

3. Scared   _____

4. Poor   _____

5. Disorganized   _____

6. Rut   _____

7. Addiction   _____

8. False Teeth   _____

9. Dominate   _____

10. Flirtatious   _____

Compare your answers to the author's responses in the Appendix.

For more information about choosing the right words to become more persuasive, read *Writing Persuasively,* by Kathleen Begley, a Crisp Series book by Thomson Learning.

Phrase Your Words for a Business Context

Words always exist in context. Few words are good or bad in themselves. A listener's understanding of what is meant depends on the speaker's intentions and appropriate phrasing for the context.

You can communicate more effectively in business if you phrase your statements and questions according to the adjectives brought to mind with the letters in the term face-to-face. Think of this as an acronym for the following words:

F rank	T actful	F eelings-Oriented
A ttentive	O ptimistic	A ccountable
C ourteous		C larifying
E nergizing		E xact

Using FACE-TO-FACE in Business Communication

Remembering the adjectives of the FACE-TO-FACE acronym as you phrase your statements and questions will help rather than harm your business communication, as the following examples make clear:

Frank

In business organizations, you are generally better off giving people information directly rather than trying too hard to avoid hurting someone's feelings. If you are a supervisor or manager, you must be certain that your words convey appropriate urgency and consequences without being vague, indirect, or overly harsh.

Harmful: It would be nice if we can resolve this issue today.
Helpful: We need to resolve this issue today.

Attentive

You will irritate your co-workers if you often send the message that you are too busy to deal with their concerns. Express outright your desire to extend yourself and your time.

Harmful: I'm busy; cut to the chase.
Helpful: I want to understand your viewpoint; tell me more.

Courteous

Treat people in the workplace the way you would a favorite family member or neighbor. "Please," "thank you," and "congratulations" can work wonders in this impersonal age.

Harmful: Joe, I'm really busy now. Do you have an appointment?
Helpful: Hi, Joe. Thanks for coming in. Good to see you this morning.

Energizing

One of the most common flaws in business communication is thinking that other people will understand how your idea or directive will benefit them—and thus will be motivated to follow your instructions. Most will not. You need to be explicit with your listeners or readers by using words such as "benefits," "advantages," and "payoffs" from the other person's viewpoint.

Harmful: Do this task right now.
Helpful: I need you to do this task now so we can all benefit by going home at 5 P.M.

Tactful

When a work problem arises, resist the temptation to launch an attack on the person you think is responsible. Use words that show you want to hear the other person's side of the story before you come to any conclusions.

Harmful: You idiot, you really messed up that job.
Helpful: I need to understand everything that happened.

Optimistic

Human beings frequently express ideas in transgressions and punishment. The irony is you can make the same point in a positive fashion by flipping your ideas to performance and reward.

Harmful: If you do not meet your sales quota, you will not be going to Disneyworld.
Helpful: If you meet your sales quota, you will win a trip to Disneyworld.

Feelings-Oriented

Like many people, you may be one who prefers to ignore or suppress your feelings rather than talk about them. This is okay—for you. But when other people show emotion in the workplace, it is wise to empathize rather than to judge.

Harmful: I think you're too sensitive.
Helpful: I hear you. If I were you, I'd be upset too.

Accountable

In any negative situation, avoid starting sentences with the word you. Instead, focus on I. This switch makes you sound more accountable and less accusatory.

Harmful: You shipped the stuff late again, didn't you?
Helpful: I'm really upset about the late shipment.

Clarifying

Never assume that you have understood precisely what another person has said. Develop a habit of rephrasing what you have heard and then checking for accuracy.

Harmful: I know what you're going to say before you say it.
Helpful: Did I get that right? Am I understanding you?

Exact

Too often business people talk in vague terms yet think their listeners are receiving the specifics. They may not be. Use words involving size, shape, brand, names, and location to get your message across in its entirety—especially if you want the other person to take action.

Harmful: Order the computer.
Helpful: Please order a Dell 486 computer from our regular vendor.

COMPARE THESE SENTENCES

Read the sentences below. Using the meaning of the letters in FACE-TO-FACE as spelled out previously, select the adjective that describes each sentence:

F rank   **T** actful   **F** eelings-Oriented

A ttentive   **O** ptimistic   **A** ccountable

C ourteous   **C** larifying

E nergizing   **E** xact

1. I want to meet with you at 3 P.M. in my office to discuss your lateness to the meeting this morning.

   _____

2. Your ideas are very interesting; please continue.

   _____

3. Hello, Sally. Please have a seat. How are you today?

   _____

4. Believe me, you'll benefit from serving on this committee at evaluation time.

   _____

5. Everyone makes mistakes; but in this case, I need to know the details.

   _____

6. If you communicate well face-to-face, you'll be successful.

   _____

7. I can see why you're upset.

   _____

CONTINUED

8. I apologize; I let your order fall through and it never got recorded.

   _____

9. Let's make sure we all have the same understanding.

   _____

10. Would you get me an 8 oz. black coffee from the cafeteria?

    _____

Compare your answers to the author's responses in the Appendix.

Update Your Language

Although organizational structures and values have changed dramatically since the 20th century, you may be among the majority of people who have not yet updated your language accordingly. Consequently, your messages may fail to match today's circumstances. Consider the following shifts in economic status and management styles in recent years:

20th Century	21st Century
Industrial economy	Information economy
Top-down management	Bottom-up management
Paternalistic policies	Shareholder-driven policies
Bureaucratic procedures	Intrapreneurial procedures
Bloated work forces	Lean-and-mean staffing
Homogeneous labor force	Diverse labor force
Company focus	Customer focus
Formal atmosphere	Casual atmosphere
National perspective	Global perspective
Slow decision making	Fast decision making

Shifting Patterns in Everyday Business Discourse

The following are examples of how these shifting patterns might emerge in face-to-face conversations in a typical workplace. As you read these comments, imagine that they are being spoken by managers and employees of a computer company called ABC Software.

Information Economy

Old-Fashioned: We need to research in the library.
Modern: We have the information right here in our database.

Bottom-Up Management

Old-Fashioned: Let's go with the vice president's idea.
Modern: I think we should talk to employees on the shop floor.

Shareholder-Driven Policies

Old Fashioned: The company will take care of our long-term employees.
Modern: The company needs to downsize to raise stock prices.

Intrapreneurial Procedures

Old Fashioned: We've always done it this way.
Modern: It's time we tried something new—even if it's risky.

Lean Staffing

Old-Fashioned: Let's assign 25 people to the project.
Modern: I think five people can complete this project.

Diverse Labor Force

Old-Fashioned: Our Christmas party will be Dec. 19.
Modern: Our new-year party will be Jan. 19.

Customer Focus

Old-Fashioned: We offer only off-the-shelf software.
Modern: We can customize any software for your specific needs.

Casual Atmosphere

Old-Fashioned: Mr. Jones, your assistance is appreciated.
Modern: Joe, thanks for your help.

Global Perspective

Old-Fashioned: Our sales are finally rising on the West Coast.
Modern: We are finally penetrating the Asian market.

Fast Decision Making

Old-Fashioned: The board must give this idea more thought.
Modern: We need to move right now.

MATCH YOUR WORDS TO THE TIMES

Read the following sentences in light of information about changing communications in the workplace. Write in the blank provided whether the statement sounds old-fashioned (O) or modern (M).

_____ 1. It's going to take at least three months to plan this project.

_____ 2. There's no need to ask people on the factory floor.

_____ 3. Our employees are extremely loyal; they stay for life.

_____ 4. Why fix something that's not broken?

_____ 5. We have all the money, time, and people we want.

_____ 6. Our diversity council meets every month.

_____ 7. Customers are not an interruption; they are the reason we exist.

_____ 8. Why don't we work through this issue over coffee after work?

_____ 9. How will this product sell in the international market?

_____ 10. If we don't move fast, the opportunity will the gone.

Compare your answers to the author's responses in the Appendix.

Review

Put a check (✓) in the box next to the ideas from this part that you plan to use in your work life:

❑ Value the power of words for better and for worse.

❑ Choose positive words and expressions.

❑ Send my verbal messages in a FACE-TO-FACE manner:

  ➤ **F**rank
  ➤ **A**ttentive
  ➤ **C**ourteous
  ➤ **E**nergizing
  ➤ **T**actful
  ➤ **O**ptimistic
  ➤ **F**eelings-Oriented
  ➤ **A**ccountable
  ➤ **C**larifying
  ➤ **E**xact

❑ Update my language to match 21st century economic and social trends.

P A R T 4

Listen Closely

RATE YOUR LISTENING

Assess your listening habits by placing a check (✓) by the statements that reflect behaviors you regularly do. Then count the number of check marks you have made:

❑ 1. Find a quiet place to conduct business.

❑ 2. Close the door to filter unnecessary noise.

❑ 3. Send telephone callers to voice mail during face-to-face meetings.

❑ 4. Tell others to interrupt you only in case of emergency.

❑ 5. Turn off radios, CD players, or other distracting noise.

❑ 6. Arrange for comfortable face-to-face seating for everyone.

❑ 7. Provide coffee or refreshments if a meeting is going to be long.

❑ 8. Set the thermostat slightly lower than usual.

❑ 9. Consider going for a walk to talk privately.

❑ 10. Get enough sleep so you will not be fatigued.

❑ 11. Avoid scheduling meetings right before lunch or quitting time.

❑ 12. Clear your mind of thoughts other than the matter at hand.

❑ 13. Acknowledge but put aside any biases or prejudices you may have.

❑ 14. Stay open-minded to new ideas and statements.

❑ 15. Admit that you cannot know everything on a topic even if you are an expert.

❑ 16. Watch facial expression and body language of other speakers.

❑ 17. Sit up straight, maintain eye contact, and stay alert.

❑ 18. Say "focus" to yourself if you find your mind wandering.

❑ 19. Squelch the urge to interrupt.

❑ 20. Strive to learn something new in every conversation.

If you checked 16–18, this is excellent. Bravo! If you checked 11–15 items, you have some good listening habits, but there is room for improvement. If you checked fewer than 10, then pay special attention to this part for ways to develop and enhance your ability to listen.

Enhance Your Listening Ability

According to many studies, most people listen at about 25% of their potential, which means they ignore, forget, distort, or misunderstand 75% of what they hear. But lazy listening habits can be costly, to business and to you.

A common contributor to poor listening is barriers. Some are internal, such as impatience to go to lunch. Others are external, such as a jackhammer on the street outside.

Business people sometimes fail to use their common sense to remedy these problems. Sometimes the solution is as simple as moving your physical location or asking noisemakers to quiet down.

Master the Five-Point Technique

Once you have developed a positive attitude and set up a space conducive to conversation, you will become a better listener by following these five points:

1. Give nonverbal feedback
2. Delay your response
3. Paraphrase and clarify
4. Affirm the speaker's feelings
5. Suggest options rather than give orders

Please note that none of these points recommends giving suggestions or providing solutions. You should offer advice only if a person specifically asks for it. Most people want a sounding board rather than your words of wisdom, however profound they may be.

REMOVE THE BARRIER

Read the list of common barriers to good listening. Use the blank provided for each one to describe a way to remedy the problem:

1. Your colleague has a heavy Russian accent.

   _____

2. People are laughing and talking outside your office.

   _____

3. A loud rock 'n' roll tune is playing on a nearby CD.

   _____

4. It is almost time for lunch.

   _____

5. Seminar participants are having an afternoon slump.

   _____

6. A Japanese woman is speaking very softly.

   _____

7. The phone rings several times during a meeting.

   _____

8. Your co-worker sharing your office cubicle loudly slurps soda through a straw.

   _____

9. Several announcements are broadcast over the loudspeaker.

   _____

10. Everyone is talking at the same time.

    _____

Compare your answers to the author's responses in the Appendix.

Give Nonverbal Feedback

When you hear the term *body language,* you probably think of the facial expressions and body gestures you make as a *speaker.* But nonverbal cues are even more important when you are the *listener.* One of the easiest yet little-used techniques to impress your supervisors is to appear to be engrossed in their every word when they are making presentations.

Spot the Signals

From the responses below, check (✓) those that probably would be taken as positive by a speaker watching your reaction:

- ❑ 1. Sighing
- ❑ 2. Looking out the window
- ❑ 3. Leaning forward
- ❑ 4. Twirling your hair
- ❑ 5. Nodding
- ❑ 6. Slumping
- ❑ 7. Tapping your foot
- ❑ 8. Answering the phone
- ❑ 9. Smiling
- ❑ 10. Avoiding eye contact

No doubt you recognized that only 3, 5, and 9 would be taken as positive signals by someone who was speaking with you. The others send a general message that you are not really engaged in the conversation or presentation taking place. To improve your listening ability, start paying attention to the nonverbal feedback you may be giving without even realizing it.

Delay Your Response

Many of today's adults grew up at a time when it was commonplace for teachers to give a pop quiz, to test students unexpectedly. To avoid classroom embarrassment in such a situation, you may have developed the habit of having a ready answer. But this can lead to speaking prematurely, one of the hallmarks of poor listening.

"One big clue that we aren't really focused on what someone is saying is how quickly we respond after he has finished speaking," says Matthew Gilbert in *Communication Miracles at Work.* "When a person is talking, it doesn't mean we use the time to figure out what to say next. It's just the opposite; we use the time to listen."

Here are some tips to improve your comfort with delayed response:

➤ Ask speakers at the outset of a conversation if they want feedback—or just to be listened to.

➤ Focus intently with both your eyes and your ears.

➤ Take notes on key points said.

➤ When there is a pause, count to five before speaking.

➤ Before you speak, ask the person if he has more to say.

➤ Wait for the other person to respond before you jump back into the conversation.

➤ Sit back and listen; you do not have to solve everyone's problems.

Paraphrase and Clarify

One of the best ways to show a speaker that you are listening is to repeat back what the person has said. Huh? To be sure, paraphrasing can seem repetitious. Many studies show, however, that it makes speakers feel appreciated. You may benefit from using a two-part technique in which you (1) explain why you are paraphrasing, and (2) repeat back what you have just heard. Let's look at each of these steps in more detail.

Step 1: Explain Your Reasons for Paraphrasing

Head off any potential offense the other person might take by explaining your reasons for paraphrasing what she has just said. Often you can create good feelings by saying something like the following:

➤ Your ideas are important to me; let me feed them back to you.

➤ I want to make sure I'm understanding you; here's what I heard you say.

➤ I think I have everything clear, but let me paraphrase just to make certain.

➤ Let me go over your key points again because I want to have the facts correct.

➤ Would you mind listening while I repeat your main points just to make sure I got everything straight?

➤ I think you said the following.

➤ You seem to make several key points; I'd like to enumerate them for accuracy's sake.

Step 2: Put the Other Person's Ideas in Your Own Words

Rather than repeating verbatim what the other person just said, put the ideas into your own words. This effort shows that you have truly heard and digested his concerns. Here are some examples:

Original: I'm really upset about not getting a higher evaluation this year.
Paraphrase: You're disappointed in the results of your annual appraisal.

Original: If I don't get a larger office, I'm quitting.
Paraphrase: You feel a larger office is so important that you might quit if you don't get one.

Original: I think I'm doing most of the work for my team.
Paraphrase: You think your team is letting you down on the workload.

Original: My mother is dying and I'm grief-stricken.
Paraphrase. You're under a lot of stress because your mom is very ill.

Original: I want to go on flex time so I can cut down on my commuting time.
Paraphrase. You think that you could cut down on your commuting time if the company could arrange flex time.

Original: I need a faster computer to get my work done.
Paraphrase: You're saying that a computer upgrade would make you more productive.

Original: I'd like a three-month leave of absence to take care of my ailing sister.
Paraphrase. You want a 90-day leave to help your sister.

Affirm the Speaker's Feelings

Most people want you to acknowledge and affirm their feelings, however intense those emotions may be. You make a big mistake as a listener when you negate a person's self-worth by saying, "Well, you shouldn't feel that way," or "That feeling is stupid." This advice is especially true when you are dealing with customers, external or internal.

Here are some ways to affirm the emotion often involved in heated exchanges—without necessarily agreeing with the other individual.

➤ I can understand why you'd be upset.

➤ If I were you, I'd be angry too.

➤ I'm sure you have better things to do than go round and round on this issue.

➤ What a dreadful experience!

➤ I'm so sorry for the trouble this matter has caused you.

➤ It's natural to feel angry sometimes.

➤ I hear the distress in your voice.

Because of childhood socialization against expressing so-called negative emotions such as anger and fear, most people are nervous after pouring their heart out to another individual. So, by affirming rather than criticizing speakers' feelings, you help them feel safe and willing to continue talking. This technique results in your learning more about any situation and getting closer to a satisfactory conclusion.

FEEL THEIR PAIN

Read the following statements. Check (✓) the ones that would make a person put aside anger and come around to your way of thinking:

❑   1. I hear what you're saying, but you're wrong.

❑   2. I've heard this story a thousand times before.

❑   3. Get over it.

❑   4. If your attitude were more positive, you wouldn't feel so angry.

❑   5. I think you're overreacting.

❑   6. For gosh sakes, it's not life or death.

❑   7. Are you on medication?

❑   8. The same thing happened to me and I didn't complain.

❑   9. I really don't see the problem, or why you're so mad.

❑ 10. It's only money.

Compare your answers to the author's responses in the Appendix.

Suggest Options

A common thread in most tips on listening is accepting that most people can solve their own problems. Rather than your opinions, reasonably intelligent men and women merely need someone to listen as they weigh options.

When you dispense advice too readily, you risk winding up in a lose-lose situation. Think about it. If a person acts on your suggestions and things turn out badly, you are likely to bear the brunt of some unexpected anger. On the other hand, if your counsel is truly wise, the person may come back repeatedly for more—creating a frustrating time management issue for you.

Tempting though it may be to share your wisdom with the world, you are well served, in business communication especially, to view yourself as a sounding board. Listen closely to other people and, if asked, suggest possible options. What? And keep your valuable advice to yourself? Exactly.

MAKE THE RIGHT CHOICE

In each of the following situations, a person is venting his feelings about the stated topic. Read the possible responses that follow each situation, and circle the letter of the response that suggests an option, rather than directing what to do.

1. Car troubles
   a) You have to go to my mechanic; he's my brother-in-law.
   b) I can check under the hood or drive you to the service station.

2. Customer complaint
   a) We can give you a refund or a credit.
   b) Here's a credit on your account; that's all I can do.

3. Household chores
   a) I think you should hire a housekeeper to clean up the mess.
   b) I wonder if your spouse or your kids could help with the chores.

4. Busy schedule
   a) Have you considered asking for an assistant or a new computer?
   b) You must march into your boss's office right now and say you're overwhelmed.

5. Night school
   a) You should take fewer courses next semester.
   b) It might be wise to cut down on your course load or take easier classes next semester.

6. Missed promotion
   a) Perhaps joining more committees or documenting your work would help you get promoted next year.
   b) You ought to forget about going through channels and complain directly to Human Resources.

7. Upcoming presentation
   a) I'm certain deep breathing would help you.
   b) I find it's helpful to rehearse my speech either into a tape recorder or in front of some friends.

Compare your answers to the author's responses in the Appendix.

CASE STUDY: Hold Your Tongue

Boris is an engineer who has risen through the ranks to become manager of a 10-person organization. When he was younger, the emphasis in communication was on public speaking rather than on listening. This leads Boris often to jump into conversations with advice and solutions without really understanding the issues.

Soo Yee comes to him with a personal problem. She says she is worn out from caring for her elderly mother and her teenage children. She wonders aloud whether going part-time will negatively affect her long-range career.

Boris is in the middle of a computer spreadsheet. Without moving from behind his desk, he tells Soo Yee that she should take up such matters with Human Resources instead of bothering him. When Soo Yee continues talking about her dilemma, he jumps in with an idea: putting her mother in an assisted-living facility.

Soo Yee bursts into tears and tells Boris he is insensitive. Boris is baffled because he was sincere in trying to advise Soo Yee.

Write a script in which Boris responds effectively to Soo Yee using the five-point technique, as follows:

1. Start with nonverbal feedback.

2. Delay your response.

3. Paraphrase and clarify.

4. Affirm the speaker's feelings.

5. Give options, not recommendations, as you see them.

Compare your script to the author's in the Appendix.

Review

Put a check (✓) in the box next to the ideas from this part that you plan to use in your work life:

❑ Assess my listening habits on a regular basis.

❑ Memorize components of the five-point listening format

❑ Show interest as a listener by my body language.

❑ Postpone my response to speakers until they are finished talking.

❑ Clarify what I have heard by rephrasing.

❑ Respect the emotions of speakers, even irritating ones.

❑ Give people alternatives, not advice, unless asked.

Communicate

Across the Miles

"*I can believe we can change the world if we start talking to one another again.*"

——**Margaret Wheatley**, *Turning to One Another: Simple Conversations to Restore Hope for the Future*

Adapt Face-to-Face Strengths to Other Communication

In high-priority situations or those involving significant conflict, emotion, authority, and money, face-to-face communication is the ideal. Other modes of communication just do not provide the team-building opportunities that meeting in person can. Relationships grow when meeting participants can have spontaneous conversations during breaks, at meals, or even in the hotel exercise room in the off hours.

Sometimes it is simply not practical to get everyone together in the same place for an in-person meeting. Instead, the participants must adapt the strengths of face-to-face communication to the other modes available to them, whether these are the telephone, teleconferencing, videoconferencing, or e-mail.

A common business mistake is to think that body language, appearances, voice quality, time, and spatial relationships count little, if at all, during remote business contacts. The truth is that some of these factors—especially voice quality—are more important in remote encounters than they are in person.

Effective electronic communication, like speaking face-to-face, depends on effective nonverbal behaviors. Remember, your words account for less than 10% of typical messages. The following sections suggest ways to apply the best features of face-to-face communication, specifically nonverbals, when you are unable to get together in person.

Telephone

> **Body Language:** Smile. Smiling transmits energy and enthusiasm, even though the person on the other end cannot see you. Research shows that telephone users feel more comfortable talking to people who are smiling than to those who are not.

> **Voice:** Speak in an upbeat tone. Because others are unable to see you on the telephone, voice plays an even more powerful part here than it does in face-to-face encounters. Breathe from your diaphragm and speak in low octaves.

> **Time:** Watch the clock. Being sensitive to busy schedules or time zone differences makes for good telephone manners. People eight to 12 time zones away, for example, do not want to stay up in the middle of the night to speak with colleagues halfway around the world.

> **Positioning/Surroundings:** Go to a quiet place. If your telephone is in a busy, noisy area, it will negatively affect your ability to send and receive accurate messages. Create a good listening environment. This is especially important if you are using a cellular phone in a location with background noise or poor reception. Move around if it's practical. Walking while on the telephone eases tension and makes you sound more authoritative. And it eliminates tremors in your voice.

Teleconference

> **Body Language:** Focus your eyes and attention in one place. If you have a habit of looking around the room while teleconferencing, stop now. It detracts from your communication, even electronically.

> **Voice:** Increase your volume. Because of the many people on the average teleconference, it is important to speak loudly and clearly. Check to make sure you can be heard at all teleconference sites.

> **Time:** Arrive at the exact hour. Most corporations hook up teleconference lines only for a limited period; extending that time creates unnecessary expense. Lateness also forces other people to waste their valuable time waiting for you.

> **Positioning/Surroundings:** Speak directly into the microphone. Sitting close to the electronic speaker helps get your point across without strain on the part of your listeners. Resist distractions, such as shuffling papers or answering e-mail, while someone else is speaking. Comfortable seating will help you maintain focus.

Videoconference

> **Body Language:** Use your eyes, face, arms and hands expressively. On videoconferences, as when on stage, your body language should be more exaggerated than when you are meeting face-to-face.

> **Voice:** Enunciate clearly. The sound on videoconferences sometimes is less than ideal. Be sure not to drop ending consonants such as "ng," "t," or "d."

> **Time:** As in teleconferences, videoconferencing requires you to be on time every time—or the lines go dead. Lateness conveys a negative message. Be sure to test the videoconference equipment before starting.

> **Positioning/Surroundings:** Line up for the camera. You should position yourself alongside other people so that everyone appears in the shot. Avoid dominating the scene.

E-mail

> **Voice:** Write conversationally. Make your writing sound as if it were coming from your voice, not from a stilted corporate manual.

> **Time:** Be brief. Keep your e-mails short and to the point. Many readers do not scroll past the first computer screen.

> **Positioning/Surroundings:** Get comfortable. Ergonomically correct desks and chairs help you concentrate on your writing rather than on your aching back.

Follow These Tips from Afar

For budget, time, travel, and other reasons, occasions certainly exist where you simply cannot get everyone together in the same place for a face-to-face meeting. The trick of remote communication is simulating the best attributes of talking and listening in person.

➤ Accept the fact that remote communication takes more energy.

➤ Discuss the inherent difficulties of distance with your reports.

➤ Emphasize that you want everyone in the loop.

➤ Acknowledge birthdays and anniversaries from afar.

➤ Ask people what mode of communication they prefer.

➤ Create an annual schedule of in-person visits.

➤ Go out of your way to see people when they are in your area.

➤ Talk to each person in your circle at least weekly.

➤ Establish a bond of trust and respect with people you can't see.

➤ Give remote people the benefit of doubt when problems arise.

➤ Be creative and memorable in bridging remote problems.

Appeal to the Senses

One of the best ways to keep up morale and productivity in long distance situations is using techniques to transcend time and space through the five human senses. Here are real-life examples of creative ways some remote workers have used to form and remain a cohesive team:

Sense	Creative Remote Communication
Sight	Create photo album of remote workers
Sound	Leave birthday messages and songs on voicemail
Smell	Mail food items associated with different locations, such as Philadelphia pretzels or Seattle coffee
Taste	Wrap and send pieces of cake from the office baby shower
Touch	Pack snowballs from Boston in ice and send to San Diego

ELECTRIFY YOUR COMMUNICATION

Read the following statements and, in the blank before each one, write *T* if the statement is true or *F* if it is false.

_____ 1. Your body language should be more exaggerated on video than in person.

_____ 2. Your office environment is irrelevant on the telephone.

_____ 3. All workers expect telephone calls to occur within business hours of the United States' eastern time zone.

_____ 4. Walking around while speaking on the phone can ease your nervousness.

_____ 5. Typing a letter is okay when someone else is speaking on a teleconference.

_____ 6. Running a spell check before sending an e-mail saves you from taking the time to proofread the entire message.

_____ 7. Nonverbal communication counts little unless you are meeting face-to-face where the other person can see you.

_____ 8. If you are the most important person speaking on the videoconference, you should position yourself in the front and center of the screen so the others are in subordinate positions.

_____ 9. Even though no one can see you in a teleconference, your communication will be more effective if you focus your attention in one place throughout the conference.

_____ 10. It is best to make e-mails sound as if you are talking to the person.

Compare your answers to the author's responses in the Appendix.

Respect Cross-Cultural Preferences

In today's global economy, telephone calls, teleconferences, videoconferences, and e-mail often involve people of different cultures than your own. This can present special challenges.

"The communications styles characteristic of given cultures are often distinctly different," writes Dale Leathers in *Successful Nonverbal Communication.* "To communicate successfully with members of another cultural group, we must be able to identify those behaviors that define a unique communication style of the culture."

Acknowledge Differing Norms

Cultural diversity experts have identified a series of norms that differ in various societies. Some of these distinctions are listed below. As you may recognize, the United States generally embraces the attitudes in the left-hand column while other nations or cultures lean toward the values in the right-hand column.

United States	Other Nations
Egalitarian	Hierarchal
Individualistic	Group-Oriented
Direct	Indirect
Time Focus	Relationship Focus
Conflict Management	Harmony
Change	Tradition
Strict Time	Elastic Time
Competition	Cooperation
Extroversion	Introversion
Future View	Past View

There are, of course, many exceptions and differences within the same culture. Be careful not to stereotype entire populations with the same values and traits.

Communicate Across Cultures

So what does all this mean in communication with those of another culture, whether in person or through electronic means? Simply this: You may want to adapt the content of your message to be more appealing to your international co-workers, customers, and suppliers.

American-born individuals, for example, might want to be less direct with those of other cultures than they would be with their fellow nationals. People of other cultures may want to flex toward the American penchant for brevity. The point is not to abandon nationalistic and ethnic preferences. It is to increase cross-cultural effectiveness.

Here are examples of how you can transmit the same message to appeal to different cultures:

Egalitarian: Let's get started on the project right now.
Hierarchal: I think we should check with the company president before we start this project.

Individualistic: Thank you so much. I worked really hard to earn the promotion.
Group-Oriented: I never would have been promoted without the hard work of my team.

Direct: You need to improve your writing skills by your next performance review.
Indirect: Employees with good writing skills go far in this company.

Time Focus: I must leave the family party to get to work on time.
Relationship Focus: I can be a little late for work; it is important to socialize with my extended family and to avoid making them think I value my job more than them.

Conflict Management: Let's hash this out right now.
Harmony: Facing conflict is uncomfortable, just let the matter go.

Change: We need to downsize immediately, starting with the highest-paid staff members.
Tradition: We must show respect to our senior colleagues during the downsizing, even though many of them will be losing their jobs.

Strict Time: I can meet with you at 9 A.M.
Elastic Time: Any time in the morning is fine for our meeting.

Competition: Our team is faster than all the others.
Cooperation: Let's help the other teams get up to speed.

Extroversion: Off the top of my head, here are some ideas to write on the flip chart to get this brainstorming session started.
Introversion: I would like time to think carefully before expressing my ideas in a brainstorming session.

Future View: The company should make double-digit profits next year.
Past View: The company may return next year to its high profits from the 1990s if it follows the policies and procedures that have made us great for more than 100 years.

Gesture with Care

If you work in a multinational organization, occasionally you may travel abroad to communicate face-to-face with colleagues. When you do, you would be well advised to learn in advance about the meaning of gestures in other cultures. They often differ dramatically from your own. What you may regard as an innocent gesture in your native land may be considered utterly obscene overseas.

Although it is risky to generalize about entire societies, you should be especially aware of physical taboos, many of which involve the hands and the feet.

Consider These Customs

Read the following statements involving the meaning of gestures in other cultures. Circle whichever option in parentheses you think is the correct answer. Then check the correct responses in the Appendix.

1. You should never touch a person's head—even a child's—in (Peru, India) because it is considered the seat of the soul.

2. When beckoning in (China, Columbia), you should put your palm down and wave all the fingers toward the body.

3. In (Argentina, Russia), a pat on the shoulder is considered a sign of friendship and respect.

4. You may hold hands publicly with someone of your own gender in (Indonesia, the United States) without anyone inferring a particular sexual orientation.

5. A backward tilt of the head means "I forgot" in (Norway, Paraguay).

6. Blowing your nose in public is considered extremely bad manners in (Ireland, Korea).

7. You ought not to wink at a person of any gender in (Belgium, Taiwan).

8. In the (African, Arab) world, the left hand is considered unclean and should not be used in greeting or eating.

9. You will be considered uncouth in (Saudi Arabia, Nigeria) if you show the sole of your shoe in public.

10. In (El Salvador, England), you should never point your finger at anyone because it is considered extremely rude.

11. If someone sucks his thumb during your sales presentation in (the Netherlands, Australia), it means he does not believe your claims.

12. Business people in (Norway, Congo) will consider you overly casual if you stand with your hands in your pockets.

13. In (Sri Lanka, South Africa), signals for agreement are reversed from those in western countries, with a nod of your head up and down meaning no and a shaking of your head from side to side meaning yes.

14. It is extremely rude in (Spain, Turkey) to cross your arms while facing someone.

15. If an associate in (Morocco, Germany) holds up his thumb in a tavern, it means he is ordering one drink.

Learn Language Differences

English has become the global language—the dominant communications vehicle used in international trade, science, technology, and travel. But that does not mean that anyone who knows English is able to understand you.

The English that non-Americans learn is most often British English, which means that many American words and phrases may be unfamiliar in the global marketplace. As George Bernard Shaw once noted, "England and America are two countries divided by a common language." Thus, it is useful to learn differences and be prepared to explain words or phrases that you thought were universal.

Americanize That Word

In *Do's and Taboos of Using English Around the World,* Roger Axtell provides many examples of British English vs. American English as in the following statements. See if you know the definition of the following italicized words and phrases as they are commonly used in the United Kingdom, as opposed to the United States.

1. A *perambulator* is a (baby carriage, crutch).

2. *Washing up* means to (get a bath, do the dishes).

3. The *wing* of a car is the (roof, fender)

4. If a man is wearing *garters*, it means he has on (a necktie, suspenders)

5. A *torch* is a (match, flashlight)

6. Londoners often wear *wellies*, which are (hats, boots)

7. Moviegoers often *queue up*, which means (eat popcorn, stand in line)

8. In buildings in the United Kingdom, the *first floor* is the (ground floor, floor directly above the ground level).

9. A *biro* is a (special beer, ballpoint pen).

10. Dual-career couples sometimes hire *chars*, which are (housecleaners, nannies).

Compare your answers to the author's responses in the Appendix.

Avoid Idiomatic Speech

American English, like any language, is filled with idioms—sayings peculiar to a people or to a given community. Such words and phrases are second nature to native speakers of a language. But they rarely are taught in the classroom.

Using American English idioms in other English-speaking countries or with non-native speakers can lead to linguistic misunderstanding, confusion, and embarrassment. The solution is to speak in standard words and phrases. Potentially problematic usages include the following categories:

Acronyms: Words formed from the initials or initial parts of the words in compound terms, such as OSHA (Occupational Safety and Health Administration) and NIMBY (not in my backyard).

Confusing: My IRA is growing.
Clear: My Individual Retirement Account (IRA) is growing.

Doublespeak: Language used to deceive usually through concealment or misrepresentation of the truth.

Confusing: The company is experiencing negative cash flow.
Clear: The company is losing money.

Euphemisms: Agreeable or inoffensive expressions substituted for words that may offend or suggest something unpleasant.

Confusing: I'm going to the restroom.
Clear: I'm going to use the toilet.

Figures of Speech: A form of expression used to convey meaning or heighten effect often by identifying one thing with another that has a meaning or connotation familiar to the reader or listener.

Confusing: Let's take a seventh-inning stretch.
Clear: Let's take a break.

Jargon: The technical, obscure, and often pretentious language or terminology of a special activity or group.

Confusing: We are committed to providing strategic, results-based solutions that improve your bottom line.
Clear: We show you how to make more money.

Oxymoron: A combination of seemingly contradictory or incongruous ideas.

Confusing: The president is taking a working vacation.
Clear: The president will do some work while he is away.

Regionalisms: Sayings specific to a geographical area

Confusing: Y'all come back now, ya hear?
Clear: Please come back again.

CLEAR THE AIR

Read the following memo from a sales manager to her staff. Underline idioms that might be puzzling to non-American speakers of English. Then rewrite the memo using plain language that would be clearer to all readers.

Memo to Staff

I don't believe in holding bad news close to the vest. So I'm not going to beat around the bush. Sales last quarter went down the toilet. I mean we hit rock bottom. We have to get our acts together. Quite frankly, I need sales to go through the roof this quarter or all our heads will be on the block. The president of the company keeps his eye on the bottom line and he is fit to be tied about our anemic results. He is singing the blues at every meeting of the company bigwigs. So suit up and do one for the Gipper. We need desperately to get a leg up on our competition and get into the black. Otherwise, as flashy new competitors come down the pike with the next new thing, we will be dead in the water.

_____

_____

_____

_____

_____

_____

_____

_____

_____

_____

Compare your answers to the author's responses in the Appendix.

Review

Put a check (✓) in the box next to the ideas from this part that you plan to use in your work life:

❑ Learn how to simulate the best face-to-face practices when communicating long distance.

❑ Use all available nonverbals on telephone calls, during teleconferences and videoconferences, and even in e-mail.

❑ Factor in cross-cultural values when communicating across the miles.

❑ Select words likely to be understood by all English speakers, both American and non-American.

❑ Avoid confusing idiomatic language such as clichés, doublespeak, and jargon.

A P P E N D I X

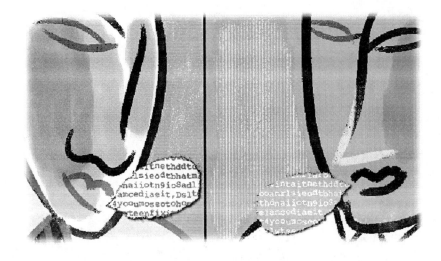

Appendix to Part 1

Comments & Suggested Responses

Face the Expressions

The correct responses are:

1. face time
2. get out of my face
3. straight face
4. about face
5. face-to-face
6. face value
7. flat on her face
8. facial expressions
9. saving face
10. two-faced
11. face the music
12. best face
13. the nose on your face
14. poker face

Recall Your Own Encounters

There is no single correct response. The following are examples that could apply in each situation:

1. Management and the union stayed together until they reached an agreement.
2. The company held face-to-face meetings with survivors of the downsizing.
3. The team set up a weekend location to finish the project.
4. I visit remote locations once a quarter because the CEO mandates it.
5. We all had classroom training to improve our customer service for the $20 million order.

Send Your Message

The correct responses are 1, 3, 4, 5, 7, 8, 10, and 12.

Differentiate the Types

The correct responses are: 1) V; 2) N; 3) V; 4) N; 5) N; 6) N; 7) N; 8) N; 9) V; 10) N. The purpose of this exercise is to demonstrate the power of nonverbal communication.

Case Study: Analyze Others' Behavior

There is no single correct response, but the following are the author's suggested responses:

1. Frank could turn to Alison and Ellis for help. Because he admires their interpersonal skills, he could ask how they developed such ease with coworkers. He would probably find out they took courses and practiced.

2. Frank could attend seminars to improve his face-to-face communication. By doing so, he would learn new abilities and also demonstrate his resolve to his manager. Frank's next performance review probably will reflect his willingness.

3. Frank should choose to pay attention to face-to-face communication because it is a key to managerial success. When technical people become team leaders, supervisors, or managers, their key responsibility is not to program computers or analyze materials. It is to motivate and inspire people, which require excellent interpersonal skills.

4. Frank could join groups outside of work, perhaps an industry trade association, to practice his face-to-face communication skills. Should anyone ask for volunteers to present information or host events, Frank could speak up.

Appendix to Part 2

Comments & Suggested Responses

Check the Lexicon

The correct responses are:

1. how you say it
2. a thousand words
3. the money
4. cheap
5. I do
6. of the soul
7. louder than words
8. your mouth is
9. cut bait
10. shut up

The fact that these phrases are so familiar demonstrates the value of the unspoken in our society.

Translate These Gestures

The correct responses depend on context, such as how exaggerated a gesture is or what other people in the room are doing. But the gestures could be read as follows:

1. lying
2. disapproval
3. accusation
4. anxiety
5. anger
6. flirtation
7. nervousness
8. separation
9. confidence
10. uncertainty
11. expertise
12. equality

Remember Your Impressions

There is no single correct response. The following are the author's suggested responses:

1. Grace Kelly: Her cool good looks and regal demeanor made her a favorite of director Alfred Hitchcock, whose movies propelled her to fame long before she married Prince Rainier of Monaco.

2. Winston Churchill: his ever-present cigar became a macho trademark during World War II, adding to his image as a bold, blunt, blustery leader.

3. Marilyn Monroe: Her blonde mane and buxom figure were keys to making her a highly successful sex symbol in the 1950s.

4. Mother Teresa. Her wrinkled face, devoid of cosmetics, tied in well with her image of simplicity and caring and helped her raise millions of dollars for charity.

5. Cary Grant: His refined appearance distinguished him from American-born film stars of his time, giving him unique opportunities to play suave European characters.

6. John F. Kennedy: His handsome good looks were credited with his win over Richard Nixon in 1960; during a televised debate, Kennedy looked calm and self-assured while Nixon perspired heavily.

7. Elvis Presley: His swiveling hips created a sensation when he appeared on the Ed Sullivan television show, setting him apart in the 1950s music scene.

8. Princess Diana: Her beauty was a key to the media coverage of her many charitable activities and made her a sympathetic figure, despite embarrassing revelations about her marriage.

9. Henry VIII: His girth contributed to his reputation as a gluttonous king of England, cementing his image in history books as a cruel, wanton leader who beheaded several wives.

10. Buddha: His rotund body is depicted on thousands of statues around the globe; his shape has become an icon in itself, instantly recognizable across many cultures.

Understand the Impact of Your Voice

There is no single correct response. The following are the author's responses:

1. Vijay is my wonderful manager, lest you had someone else in mind.
2. Vijay is my manager, lest you had any question about that.
3. Vijay is my manager, not yours or theirs.
4. Vijay is wonderful; other managers are not.
5. Vijay is my manager, lest you think we have some other relationship.

Appendix to Part 3

Comments & Suggested Responses

Quote Me on That

The following are the author's assessments of each speaker's quote:

1. Indira Gandhi helped establish her image as a peacemaker with this quote in the mid-1950s.

2. Martina Navratilova showed she was a fierce, athletic competitor by making a word play on an old adage at the height of her fame in the 1980s.

3. Jacqueline Kennedy Onassis, thought by some to be an extravagant spender out of touch with ordinary people, connected with common folks with this comment on parenting shortly before her death.

4. Charles De Gaulle created a dim-witted image of himself by this needless hyperbole about China in the 1950s.

5. Amelia Earhart, in an era when women pilots were out of the ordinary, said this to explain her interest in aviation.

6. Marion Barry, a controversial figure in American politics convicted at one time of cocaine abuse, did little for his image in the 1990s with this absurd comment about his city's crime rate.

7. Golda Meir, one of the oldest world leaders of her era, showed grace and humility in the 1970s when describing her feelings about aging.

8. George W. Bush, well-known for his many remarks bungling normal syntax, added fodder for comedians in this quote about children and firearms.

9. Beverly Sills spoke in exact accordance with her image as a fun-loving, upbeat, and eternally cheerful singer throughout the second half of the 20th century.

10. Eleanor Roosevelt was the first to make this quote about women's strength, which has often been attributed to others.

11. Oprah Winfrey helped propel herself into a new role as a leader of 21st century seminars on "Living Your Best Life," focusing on the here and now.

12. Martha Stewart, widely reviled as much as revered for her perfectionism, acknowledged her negative image with this statement after she came under scrutiny for insider stock trading.

13. Sylvester Stallone, known more for brawn than brains, made a fool of himself by putting down a literary classic when his career took off in the early 1970s.

14. Greta Garbo turned off many once-loyal fans when she uttered this statement upon her retirement at the height of her fame in 1941.

Speak Positively

There is no single correct response. The following are the author's responses:

1. careful
2. misunderstanding
3. cautious
4. disadvantaged
5. spontaneous
6. slump
7. habit
8. dentures
9. influence
10. friendly

Compare These Sentences

The correct response is that all sentences follow the FACE-TO-FACE format in exact order: frank, attentive, courteous, energizing, tactful, optimistic, feelings-oriented, accountable, clarifying, and exact.

Match Your Words to the Times

The correct responses are 1) O; 2) O; 3) O; 4) O; 5) O; 6) M; 7) M; 8) M; 9) M; 10) M.

Appendix to Part 4

Comments & Suggested Responses

Remove the Barrier

There is no single correct response. The following are the author's responses:

1. Learn English pronunciation difficulties commonly faced by Russians, such as distinguishing "w" and "v."
2. Close the door, ask the people to lower their voice, or move to another area
3. Turn down the CD.
4. Adjourn until the afternoon.
5. Give seminar participants a break.
6. Get physically closer to the Japanese woman or ask her to speak up.
7. Let voice mail take your calls; if possible, turn off the ringer.
8. Ask the person not to slurp so loudly.
9. Take your meeting outside.
10. Set up a speaking order or ask people not to talk over others.

Feel Their Pain

None of these responses would help diffuse a person's anger; they would likely make the matter worse.

Make the Right Choice

The correct responses are 1) b; 2) a; 3) b, 4) a, 5) b; 6) a; 7) b.

Case Study: Hold Your Tongue

There is no single correct response. The following is the author's suggested script for Boris to follow:

Before he speaks, Boris should stop working on the spreadsheet and come out from behind the desk. Rather than interrupting Soo Yee, he should delay his response, uttering only the occasional "umm" or "uh huh" as she speaks. When she is finished, Boris could say something like:

"You have your hands full with being a caregiver, but you're concerned that going part-time might hurt your career. If I were in the same situation, I would feel torn too. Have you explored other options? Perhaps you could hire in-home care for your mother and children or take a brief leave of absence to sort things out."

Appendix to Part 5

Comments & Suggested Responses

Electrify Your Communication

The correct responses are 1) true; 2) false; 3) false, 4) true, 5) false, 6) false; 7) false, 8) false, 9) true, 10) true.

Consider These Customs

The correct responses are:

1. India
2. China
3. Argentina
4. Indonesia
5. Paraguay
6. Korea
7. Taiwan
8. Arab
9. Saudi Arabia
10. El Salvador
11. Netherlands
12. Norway
13. Sri Lanka
14. Turkey
15. Germany

Americanize That Word

The correct responses are:

1. baby carriage
2. do the dishes
3. fender
4. suspenders
5. flashlight
6. boots
7. stand in line
8. the floor directly above the ground level
9. ballpoint pen
10. housecleaners

Clear the Air

The idioms in the memo (and their corresponding meanings) are:

Close to the vest	Keeping secrets
Beat around the bush	Avoid a troubling topic
Down the toilet	Fell significantly
Hit rock bottom	Performed really badly
Get our acts together	Organize and sell
Go through roof	Increase
Heads on the block	Jobs threatened
Bottom line	Profit or loss
Fit to be tied	Enraged
Anemic	Poor
Singing the blues	Complaining
Bigwigs	Executives
Suit up	Get ready
Do one for the Gipper	Make me look good
Leg up	Sell more than
Into the black	Become profitable
Come down the pike	Go into business
Dead in the water	Out of business

Here is how the memo could be rewritten:

I don't believe in keeping bad news secret. So I'm not going to avoid a troubling topic. Sales last quarter fell significantly. I mean we performed really badly. We have to organize and sell. Quite frankly, I need sales to increase this quarter or all our jobs will be threatened. The president of the company keeps his eye on profit and loss, and he is enraged about our poor results. He is complaining at every meeting of the company executives. So get ready and make me look good. We need desperately to sell more than our competition and become profitable. Otherwise, as flashy new competitors come into the business with the next new thing, we will be out of business.

Additional Reading

Axtell, Roger. *Do's and Taboos of Using English Around the World.* New York: Wiley, 1995.

Begley, Kathleen. *Writing Persusively.* Boston, MA: Thomson Learning, 2002.

Bender, Peter, and Robert Tracz. *Secrets of Face-to-Face Communication.* Toronto: Stoddart, 2001.

Bonet, Diana. *The Business of Listening.* Crisp Series, 2001.

Brehony, Kathleen. *Living a Connected Life.* New York: Owl Books, 2003

Cole, Kris. *The Complete Idiot's Guide to Clear Communication.* Indianapolis, IN: Alpha Books, 2000.

Decker, Bert. *Communication Skills for Leaders.* Boston, MA: Thomson Learning, 2006.

Dimitrius, Jo-Ellan, and Mark Mazzarella. *Reading People.* New York: Ballantine Books, 1999.

Finney, Martha. *Find Your Calling, Love Your Life.* New York: Simon & Schuster, 1998

Gilbert, Matthew. *Communication Miracles at Work.* Berkeley, CA: Conari Press, 2002.

Guerrero, Laura, Joseph DeVito, and Michael Hecht. *The Nonverbal Communication Reader.* Prospect Heights, IL: Waveland Press, 1999.

Guffey, Mary Ellen. *Business Communication: Process and Product.* Cincinnati: Southwestern College Publishing, 1997.

Hodge, Sheida. Global Smarts*: The Art of Communicating and Deal Making Anywhere in the World.* New York: Wiley, 2002.

Ivey, Allen. *Managing Face-to-Face Communication: Survival Tactics for People and Products in the 21st Century.* Amherst, MA: Microtraining, 1995.

Kindler, Herbert. *Conflict Management.* Crisp Series, 1996.

Knapp, Mark, and Judith Hall. *Nonverbal Communication in Human Interaction.* New York: Wadsworth, 2002.

Leathers, Dale. *Successful Nonverbal Communication.* Boston: Allyn and Bacon, 1997.

Lloyd, Sam R. *Accountability.* Crisp Series, 2002.

Lloyd, Sam R., and Tina Berthelot. *Self-Empowerment. Rev. Ed..* Crisp Series, 2003.

Locker, Kitty. *Business and Administrative Communication.* New York: McGraw-Hill, 2000.

McClain, Gary, and Deborah Romaine. *The Everything Managing People Book,* Avon, MA: Adams Media, 2002.

Naisbitt, John. *Megatrends.* New York: Warner Books, 1982.

Peters, Tom. *Re-Imagine.* New York: DK Publishing, 2004.

Richmond, Virginia, and James McCroskey. *Nonverbal Behavior in Interpersonal Relations.* Boston: Allyn and Bacon, 2000.

Roebuck, Chris. *Effective Communication.* New York: AMACOM, 1998.

Simons, George. *Working Together: Succeeding in a Multicultural Organization.* Crisp Series, 2002.

Todd, Jim. *World-Class Manufacturing.* New York: McGraw-Hill, 1994

Wheatley, Margaret. *Turning to One Another: Simple Conversations to Restore Hope for the Future.* New York: Berrett-Koehler, 2002.

NOTES

NOTES

Also Available

Books • Videos • CD-ROMs • Computer-Based Training Products

Subject Areas Include:

Management

Human Resources

Communication Skills

Personal Development

Sales/Marketing

Finance

Coaching and Mentoring

Customer Service/Quality

Small Business and Entrepreneurship

Training

Life Planning

Writing

VERQ